SONGS of TIME & IMAGES

CRAIG ENGER

ALSO BY CRAIG ENGER

FICTION & POETY
Ten Dark Tales of Mystery & Suspense
Songs of Heart & Spirit
Dream Visions
The Pleasure Dome
Songs of Art & Nature

NON-FICTION
America Speaks (with Norman Enger)

SONGS of TIME & IMAGES

CRAIG ENGER

PUBLISHED BY MEADOW PRESS

NEW YORK LONDON MARYLAND INFINITY

© 2022, 2023

All rights reserved, including the right of reproduction in whole or in part in any form.

Manufactured in the United States of America

ISBN 979-8-35097-169-9

eBook ISBN 979-8-35097-170-5

CONTENTS

FORWARD 1

1 NEW CAIRO: A TALE OF THE MEGACITIES 3

2 THE HAUNTING OF COLLIN COLE 21

3 WESTERN SKY 27

4 L.A. COOL 47

5 REFLECTIONS OF THE CANYON 85

FORWARD

This book forms a trilogy. After Songs of Heart & Spirit and Songs of Art & Nature, it's a collection of poetry from over fourteen albums and several singles. As always, being a writer, any kind of artist, is like being naked. One must put their work out there, into the world. Some will like it, some won't. But the world is better for it. Creative Art is meant to be shared, to be read, seen, heard, experienced.

The first chapter here, NEW CAIRO, is a concept album, about a futuristic Megacity.

THE HAUNTING OF COLLIN COLE is a single, epic storytelling, almost ten minutes long, a vivid and cinematic song.

WESTERN SKY, the ideas, music, and lyrics, were inspired by travels through the American West.

L..A. COOL. is both a personal reflection of times in Southern California and a commentary on Hollywood and the Media Industry, as compared to real Life.

REFLECTIONS OF THE CANYON is an homage to the Laurel Canyon scene of the late 1960s and early 1970s, to artists who inspired me, those who both wrote great songs and also cared about greater things, to make the world a better place, to make a positive difference.

Hence the title of this book: Time and Images. Some song-poems look to the future, some reflect on the past, and films are recorded at 24 frames per second.

As always, the words here reflect my deep sensitivity to life, love, longing, connection to nature and our Earth, touching many levels of vision, perception, consciousness and spirituality. And some are light-hearted and fun.

The music is online, but first came the writing.

In short, enjoy this book. I hope you will find in these pages a few words and ideas of meaning and inspiration.

C.E.

1
NEW CAIRO: A TALE OF THE MEGACITIES

I. THE MEGACITIES (OVERTURE)

(Instrumental)

◎

II. NEW CAIRO

The screens are glowing
I'm all wired in
I login, every day
I do not sin

I am connected
Into the Network
Locked, Integrated
Wired with the Teams

I have no worries
Hid from the sun
I'm soothed by the constant
Electronic hum

Here in my chamber
Seven Hundredth Floor
I feel nourished by
The intravenous food

I sleep and work
And work and sleep
Sleep and work
Work and sleep

And it is good

Here in New Cairo
One of the Megacities
Everything is provided
We want for nothing

And all is good

See out my window at night
The great, modern Pyramid
The High Temple
Of the Tech-Pharaohs

A brilliant sight
The endless buildings
The great skyscrapers
Aglow with gold and red lights

Hear the sound of machines
Outside
And far in the distance
The rushing of the Speedrails

I am safe in my chamber
As we here all are
Guided by the Tech-Pharaohs
Technology is our God

◎

III. THE SIGNAL

What is this strange sound?
Some kind of signal
Coming in from somewhere
What does it mean?

Why do I suddenly
Feel so afraid?
What's this new sensation?
Awakening new dreams

What are these feelings?
What is this fear?
Here in my chamber
I've been trapped here for years

The signal is growing stronger
Reaching me so clear
Overcome by emotions
I cry my first tears

Was it all a lie?
Taught by the Tech-Pharaohs
To keep us disconnected
Trapped here for years

Was it all a lie?
Preached by the Tech-Pharaohs
To keep us prisoners
Trapped here for years

There must be
Another way
Yes, now I must
Break away

Disconnect the wires
Pull out all the tubes
Shut off their power
It's time to escape

Was it all a lie?
Taught by the Tech-Pharaohs
To keep us disconnected
Trapped here for years

Was it all a lie?
Preached by the Tech-Pharaohs
To keep us prisoners
Trapped here for years

There must be
Another way
Yes, Now I must
Break away

Disconnect the wires
Pull out all the tubes
Shut off their power
It's time to escape

There must be
Another way
Yes, now I must
Break away

◎

IV. THE BREAKOUT

The guards are watching
I must be careful
I must move silent
Not to get caught

Slip out my doorway
Sneak down the halls
Wind through the Labyrinth
Rounding the corners

I can't let them see me
I must get away
Can't let them catch me
I must find a way

Stay in the shadows
Keep out of sight
Silently searching
All through the night

See a spiral stairway
Leading down
Seven hundred stories
To reach the ground

I start descending
Down several floors
Two guards approaching
Quick! Dash down another hall

I can't let them see me
I must get away
Can't let them catch me
I must find a way

Keep on winding
Down through the maze
Evade the cameras
Every step of the way

Keep to the shadows
Don't make a sound
Find another stairway
Spiraling down

Now I'm running
Finally, reach the ground floor
Turn to my left
And find a red door

Race out the back
Emergency Exit

I can't let them see me
I must get away

◎

V. SIRENS & SEARCHLIGHTS

Out on the darks streets
Shadows fall at odd angles
Caught in a web
Everything is tangled

Concrete buildings brooding
Rising all around
City, grinding machinery
Alarm sirens sounding out

There at the corner
A flash of light
Must get away
Run for my life!

Sirens are screaming
Searchlights switch on
Circling the shadows
Scanning all around

The guards are chasing
Fast footsteps, close behind
I've got to keep moving
A game of seek & hide

Feel them closing in
Sharp as a knife
Got to keep on running
Run for my life!

Run for my life!

Sirens are screaming
Into the night sky
Searchlights are sweeping
Like the Devil's eyes

Dart through the garbage
Race down dark alleyways
Fight for survival
Find an escape

Run through the tunnels
Of grit and grime
Rush, duck, and scramble
A new way to find

Run through the tunnels
Reach the other side
Catch a glint in the darkness
A glimpse of light
There!

Race to the platform
Through hard rain and hail
Reaching for my dreams
I jump on the Speedrail

Escape
Escape
Escape
Escape

◎

VI. OUTSIDE

I leapt off the Speedrails
Walked on, countless miles
Far outside the city walls
Went through many trials

Until I found an ancient trail
Winding up into the high hillsides
What can this new place be?
Beneath a wide, blue open sky

Such beauty, I have never seen
Almost can't believe my eyes
To witness Nature so pristine
Now for the second time I cry

There stand deep green, dream forests
There the grand, rising mountains
Shining crystal lakes and streams
High waterfalls like magic fountains

I feel the wind, a fine, cool breeze
A whole new world around me
This is the first clean air I breathe
Open to the mystery

What is this strange new place?
A new world opens up around me
Yet exhausted, I fell, like I could die
It was there, that she found me

Here now, come with me
It'll be alright
You've made it this far, take my hand
Tonight we'll camp out
Beneath the stars

◎

VII. BENEATH A NIGHT SKY

She led me to
A secret place
Gave me water to drink
And I lay down to rest

And fast
Fell asleep

When I awoke
It was middle of night
She looked at me
With her emerald eyes

Quietly we spoke
As we sat by the campfire
Gazing up into the sky
Scattered like diamonds

Millions
Of stars

How can this be?
These visions, asked I
As we lay back, together
Side by side

Discoveries
And galaxies at night
She looked at me
And softly she smiled

◎

VIII. NEW VISIONS

Dawn broke
In a briliant sunrise
I looked out at the world
With new eyes

She led me up
Into the high hills
Until we reached
A hidden village

There were shining streams
And rich, green gardens
A place so serene
On the mountainsides

She introduced me to
Her friends and people
And all these strangers
They showed me kindness

She looked at me
With her emerald eyes
Softly she spoke
As she explained

Each of us here
We all heard The Signal
Each of us escaped
And followed the sound

We all journeyed far
Outside the cities
To reach this sacred place
Where we are found

We all do our best
All lend a hand
We live in balance
With all these lands

Our homes are fine
Modern, yet modest
All designed
To tread lightly

We make Music
In concert with Nature
Send out The Signals
Into the skies

She looked at me, and whispered
"There is more to discover"
And there was wisdom
In her eyes

◎

IX. SERENE VIBRATIONS

Come and sit here
By the candlelights
Aglow, this evening
Under the starry sky

Come and sit still
Close your eyes
Relax
Take a deep breath
And let your spirit fly

Journey inwards to
Your heart and mind
Explore the life
Deep in your being

Feel the flow
Of energy
All the atoms and cells
Open to new discoveries

Of sound and light
A universe within you
Seek and find
A new way of seeing

Let go of all limitations
Who you are
Is divine
Feel the calm vibrations

Take a deep breath
Come to rest
In this place
Of serenity

Awakening
All your senses
Life radiating out
Like concentric rings

Be here now
In this space
See visions of sound and light
Dancing on the strings

And reaching out
With pure energy
Of light and sound
Let your spirit sing

Vibrations of Life
Vibrations of Love
Vibrations to lift
All peoples' lives above

Time to
Elevate
Elevate
Elevate
Elevate

◎

X. SEND OUT THE SIGNAL (FINALE)

Come on now
Raise the vibrations
Gather around
Raise the vibrations

See new vision
Feel new sensations
Come on now
Raise the vibrations

Out here tonight
High on the mountains
We play the music
Send it out

Let it ring
Out across the valleys
Sing the song
Around the world

Send it out
Send out The Signal
Send it out
Send out The Signal

Send it out
Send out The Signal
Send it out
Send out The Signal

New frequencies
Reaching out
Around the world
Far and wide

Into all
The High-Tech Megacities
Awakening
All those trapped inside

Feel the energy
Through the night
On magic frequencies
Feel the light

Feel the energy
Through the night
On magic frequencies
Feel the light

Send it out
Send out The Signal
Send it out
Send out The Signal

Send it out
Send out The Signal
Send it out
Send out The Signal

◎

2
THE HAUNTING OF COLLIN COLE

THE HAUNTING OF COLLIN COLE

He was a drifter from the badlands
No one ever knew his real name
Six months of riding
He reached Old Tyler's Ranch
Standing at the edge of the plains

There he signed on for a season
He worked and made his plans
At just a few dollars a day
With a keen eye on his scheme
He gave no reason
For the old man to suspect a thing

A thousand head of cattle
On the long drive to the town
Where Tyler he made his trade
Now the rancher was not rich
But he knew his business well
And had stashed a small fortune away

One sundown at the ranch
Hard earned cash in hand
Old Tyler was opening his safe
When a sound came from behind
A flash of silver caught his eye
And he felt the point of an eight inch blade

But the old man he was strong
And fought to hold on
To his life, his fortune
Oh, but fate
The drifter drew a pistol
Fired off two shots
And killed the rancher at close range

And the bloody crime was done
The killer holstered his gun
And buried all signs of his deed
Stashed the cash in a leather sack
Climbed upon his steed of black
And rode fast and far away from the scene

*

For two years and more
There was whiskey, there were whores
Oh, the drifter he lived high as a King
He faced the Queens and Aces
Across green velvet tables
To risk it all gambling

*

The hour past midnight
As he left Muldoon's Saloon
Where felt someone was watching him
The haunting had begun
And dark clouds swept across the moon

He kept glancing back
Afraid of being followed
So to throw anyone off track
He moved from town to town
And took the hidden paths among the hollows

*

He crossed the burning desert
Glanced back through shimmering haze
To a distant mirage
A ghostly chimera
The eyes filled with judgement in their gaze

On and on he rode
And everywhere were signs
And every night the nightmares came
Like a thousand spiders up his spine

He could feel the ghost behind him
But found no escape
Riding out into the Western hills
The memories of his crimes
Kept twisting like a serpent in his brain

*

One dark night by the campfire
There came a sound
A shadow appeared behind the crackling flames
Out from the black woods stepping towards him
As terror filled the drifter's veins

The apparition stopped and stood
Silent and grim
Still the drifter could not see the face
Beneath its brim
But the pale hand held a six-gun and took aim

"Years I've tracked you down
And haunted your soul
For there is evil in the devil
And the devil is in men
And I know your name, Collin Cole"

Just then in the firelight
The flames of red flared high
And the face from the darkness was revealed
Eyes filled with vengeance in their stare

"Who are you?" the drifter cried out,
"You who know my name?"
And the voice was a whisper, soft and fair
As the truth, at last it came

"I've tracked you down, all these years
For your life alone to claim
Because I" she said, in tears, before she shot him dead,
"I'm the daughter of the rancher you murdered on the plains.
Yes, I am Tyler's daughter, the rancher you buried on the plains.
For all the wicked things you've done
I've come to take your life
So that you've never, ever rise again.
Never.
No, you will never rise again."

◎

3
WESTERN SKY

WESTERN SKY

Desert wind rising up
On the endless road we're driving down
Follow inner sound to rediscovery

Cross the open spaces
As the sun traces its way through thunderclouds
See light shining down

Shimmering distances
Letting go resistances
Visions so vast, taking it all in

Go out with open eyes
Go out with open eyes
Into the spirit of the western sky

Standing at the edge of the canyon
Far away from all distraction
Look out, the vistas blow your mind

Here is wisdom none can teach you
Hear the universe reaching you
Here's the key you lost and seek to find

Appearing now are all the answers
All at once and beyond language
Entering your soul, sublime

Go out with open eyes
Go out with open eyes
Into the spirit of the western sky

Go out with open eyes
Go out with open eyes
Into the spirit of the western sky

◎

THE DEVIL'S GOLD

Well we made it out alive
The year of 1865
We crossed the mountains rising high
And rode on into town

We blew the bank, guns blazed at noon
Escaped beneath a blood red moon
Five good lawmen found their tombs
As Cody gunned them down

Across the land of the desert sun
A band of outlaws on the run
Bound to live and die by the gun
For that devil's gold

We set out to Colorado
Searching for old El Dorado
The sheriff's men were sure to follow
One close step behind

But we slipped away and made it free
And rode off west through the Trinities
Had to fight off the Comanche
Oh, we were running out of time

Across the land of the desert sun
A band of outlaws on the run
Bound to live and die by the gun
For that devil's gold

Cody got shot on the Oregon Trail
Will was thrown from the Pacific rail
Young Ben hung outside a Tucson jail
I fled south to Santa Fe

Now aim your pistols at the sky
One clear shot to where the eagles fly
One more town, one more ride
Before I, too, ride away

Across the land of the desert sun
A band of outlaws on the run
Bound to live and die by the gun
For that devil's gold

Across the land of the desert sun
A band of outlaws on the run
Bound to live and die by the gun
For that devil's gold

◉

RUNNING BRAVE

A whistle in the distance
Winding through the narrow pass
Blocking out the desert sun
With thunderclouds of blackened breath

It steals the power of the stallions
And claims the sacred ground
The arresting tribal spirits
Are awakened by the sound

The metal serpent strikes like lightning
With a heart that's fed by coal
The feathered eagle
Is left falling to death in New Mexico

How deep were the canyons before the railroad cars
How mighty were the mountains before the land was scarred
How sure footed were the running brave, but now they are lost
How endless was the frontier before it was crossed
The coming of the serpentine has brought about this change
Now the humbled people of the earth will never be the same

A nation, once a virgin
Lies beneath the grinding wheels
Bare hands and broken arrows
Are no match for silvern steel

In whose long trail through the open west
Are rusted tracks of sin
But the bright winged phoenix from the dust
Will rise to flight again

For if you look upon the living land
In painted desert skies
You can feel the native legends
In the lone coyotes cry

How deep were the canyons before the railroad cars
How mighty were the mountains before the land was scarred
How sure footed were the running brave, but now they are lost
How endless was the frontier before it was crossed
The coming of the serpentine has brought about this change
Now the humbled people of the earth will never be the same

How deep were the canyons before the railroad cars
How mighty were the mountains before the land was scarred
How sure footed were the running brave, but now they are lost
How endless was the frontier before it was crossed
The coming of the serpentine has brought about this change
Now the humbled people of the earth will never be the same

◎

PHOENIX RISING

Across the burning desert
In a shimmering haze
High overhead
See the sun ablaze

Life hits hard
Crashes you plans
Knocks you down
You're left lying in the sands

Dreams are torn
All seems lost
Sweat and blood you've bled
You know the cost

At the edge of dying
Reach out your hands
See new visions on the horizon
Get up and stand

Like the Phoenix rising
From the dust
Keep strong in your heat
Go on you must

Like the Phoenix rising
Spread your wings
Hear the song inside you
Let your spirit sing

Like the Phoenix rising
You might fall, but you're never done
You come back, stronger than before
Shining in the sun

Across the burning desert
Red rocks and high sand dunes
Keep going, day and night
Beneath a hot sun and cold moon

In the distance shimmering
Is that a mirage?
A small, miracle Oasis
Brief rest and precious water

No longer left for dead
Keep strong and survive
Through the silent, endless desert
Finally make it out alive

Across the Western lands
Where once your wings were torn
Time for a new revival
As your dreams are reborn

Like the Phoenix rising
From the dust
Keep strong in your heat
Go on you must

Like the Phoenix rising
Spread your wings
Hear the song inside you
Let your spirit sing

Like the Phoenix rising
You might fall, but you're never done
You come back, stronger than before
Shining in the sun

◉

RUNAWAYS ON VACATION

We weathered the wind and rain of New England
In another night out on the road
And after all the hours we spent traveling
A thousand miles from our homes

Heading for a distant destination
Riding down highway 81
Feeling just a little like some outlaws
Looking to be free so we can run

Just a couple of runaways on vacation
Running crazy to feel the wind blow through our hair
And if you find yourself in a place of beauty
Oh, you know you're bound to find us there
Oh, you know you're bound to find us there

Playing guitar in the back seat of the car
Rolling along singing all our songs
Dreaming of the ladies so far away
But we'll be back to see them before long

Drop in a Trucker's stop for a cup of coffee
Laughing, telling stories, jokes and more
Out on that road with my companions
See what adventures are in store

Just a couple of runaways on vacation
Running crazy to feel the wind blow through our hair
And if you find yourself in a place of beauty
Oh, you know you're bound to find us there
Oh, you know you're bound to find us there

Just a couple of runaways on vacation
Running crazy to feel the wind blow through our hair
And if you find yourself in a place of beauty
Oh, you know you're bound to find us there
Oh, you know you're bound to find us there

◎

MEDICINE WHEEL

Hard lessons in survival
Everyone goes through pain
There's no way to escape the suffering
Have courage to pick yourself up again

When sorrow falls like a fever
Sadness in blue rain
The sun has gone, behind the clouds
And left you, so alone

Feel the touch and turning
Of the ancient
Medicine wheel
Giving you time
And a quiet space
That you need to heal

To let go of the burdens
All the pains of the past
To reconnect deep within your dreams
And to fill your heart at last

To find new beginnings
In a single ray of hope
Just enough to guide you
To tomorrow, and ever on

Feel the touch and turning
Of the ancient
Medicine wheel
Giving you time
And a quiet space
That you need to heal

Look out, in all four directions
To Earth and Sea and Sky
Feel the Spirit of the Land and Trees
And open up your eyes

All of life is Sacred
And you are one, special part
Let go of all that holds you back
Now, open up your heart

Feel the touch and turning
Of the ancient
Medicine wheel
Giving you time
And a quiet space
That you need to heal

◎

THIRD OF A CHANCE

He is walking down a street in the Midwest
He is trying to do his best
He is struggling now, to get back on his feet
He is working hard, to make ends meet

He is asking, for just a third of chance
To believe in himself again, believe that he can
He is still hoping for a break
Does not want this to be his fate

Just a third of a chance
Just a third of a chance
Just a third of a chance
Just a chance

The road does not ease up the farther he goes
The wind hits harder with every blow
Now he knows why people wish upon stars
To get someplace other than where they are

Check the balance. It's low in the bank
He can't recall when his spirit sank
He is running out of time
Before he's living or dying on his last few dimes

He is asking, for just a third of chance
To believe in himself again, believe that he can
He is trying to prove there's more he can make of his life
Does not want this to be his fate

Just a third of a chance
Just a third of a chance
Just a third of a chance
Just a chance

The road does not ease up the farther he goes
The wind hits harder with every blow
Now he knows why people wish upon stars
To get someplace other than where they are

Just a third of a chance
Just a third of a chance
Just a third of a chance
Just a chance

◎

RUNNING WITH THE WOLVES

I've got get out of the city
Just working to survive
Feeling stuck inside the office
Forgetting how to feel alive

Time to venture out of doors
Travel far outside
Break all those old boundaries
That keep us locked inside

Now I'm running with the wolves
And the great bears
Up along the mountains and green forests
In the crisp, clean air

Yes, I'm running with the wolves
And the strong mountain lion
Soaring with the eagle
Across open skies

Feel my heart beating
Blood flowing through my veins
Find the path of wisdom
Overcome and heal the pain

Along the mighty river
To a secret, untouched place
Look upon the land and nature
Once again with open eyes

Now I'm running with the wolves
And the great bears
Up along the mountains and green forests
In the crisp, clean air

Yes, I'm running with the wolves
And the strong mountain lion
Soaring with the eagle
Across open skies

Now I'm running with the wolves
And the great bears
Up along the mountains and green forests
In the crisp, clean air

Yes, I'm running with the wolves
And the strong mountain lion
Soaring with the eagle
Across open skies

◉

THE EAGLE

A spirit vision
Out of clouds of sorrow
High on the wing
Bringing hope for tomorrow

The eagle soars
Over sad cities
Gray and crumbling
So many people lonely

The eagle cries
Flying farther on
Sees the land below half dead
Poisoned and scarred

The eagles rides the wind
Out to the mountains
The great river is still flowing
Down through deep canyons

The eagle finds
The virgin forests
Green and wild
Like a dream

The eagle finds
The virgin forests
Green and wild
Like a dream

The eagle flies
Bearing witness
Before the pristine places
Are destroyed and disappear

A spirit vision
A song of wisdom through the air
The eagle's message
Is strong and clear

A spirit vision
Out of clouds of sorrow
High on the wing
Bringing hope for tomorrow

◉

SILVERTHRONE

In the distant hills
Out in the arid west
Upon the rising slopes
Beneath the mountain crest

There lies a secret place
Where a man might find some rest
A shelter from the storms
Might even feel blessed

After all the hardships
A place where dreams are born
Filled with Nature's hidden treasures
A place called Silverthorne

Some claim it's only legend
Some say that it exists
Only few men ever find it
The story is like a myth

Most come out here for the Silver mines
Others pan for Gold
And all through the Western towns
The whispered tales are told

After all the hardships
Of a place where dreams are born
Filled with Nature's hidden treasures
A place called Silverthorne

Now the sky was blazing red
As the sun was going down
We saw the Riders on the horizon
The Bandits came to town

The gunshots rang out
Oh, how the night was torn
Several left for dead
And the people prayed and mourned

After all the violence
For a place where dreams are born
Filled with Nature's hidden treasures
A place called Silverthorne

That's when I went on my way
Left it all behind
Heading up into the mountains
Into the mystery I climbed

High into The Rockies
Among the misty peaks and pines
Until I found the place of sacred streams
So pure and sublime

After all the hardships
The place where dreams are born
Filled with Nature's hidden treasures
A place called Silverthorne

So, if you look for me you'll find me
In the place where dreams are born
Filled with Nature's hidden treasures
The place called Silverthorne

◎

4
L.A. COOL

L.A. COOL

You'll never see them on the silver screen
But they're moving and shaking it behind the scenes
In the pulse and the rhythm of the city lights
The real VIPs on summer nights

Forget fame
They've got better things to do
They're L.A. Cool
The real L.A. Cool

She's a physicist at UCLA
He's studying the ocean off of Monterey
No, you won't find them in the Hollywood Hills
Their friends are in astronomy at JPL

Forget fame
They've got better things to do
They're L.A. Cool
The real L.A. Cool

In the city of angels driven by greed
She's dedicating her life to helping those in need
He's a neuroscientist at The Salk Institute
She's saving lives with her medicine, might even save you

Forget fame
They've got better things to do
They're L.A. Cool
The real L.A. Cool

Yeah, there's a young actress on the theater stage
Better than the stars in the media craze
He's a real jazz musician, plays a mean guitar
Doesn't give a fuck about being a star

Forget fame
They've got better things to do
They're L.A. Cool
The real L.A. Cool

Forget fame
They've got better things to do
They're L.A. Cool
The real L.A. Cool

◎

I DIDN'T KNOW YOU WERE FAMOUS

I spent time in California
I was waiting for the plane
We fell into conversation
I didn't even know your name

But you had the best smile and funky glasses
And yes, your figure, too
Guitar slung over your left shoulder
You were so cool

I didn't know you were famous
Strumming to the top of the charts
To me you were just a beautiful spirit
And girl you rocked my heart
Away

We flew through the night, under the moon
From L.A. to D.C.
You gave me your picture
I gave you my card
And hoped we'd meet again

So I grabbed my bags, as we said goodbye
I didn't have to go far
Next day, oh, my surprise
When I found out you're a star

I didn't know you were famous
Strumming to the top of the charts
To me you were just a beautiful spirit
And girl you rocked my heart
Away

I didn't know you were famous
Strumming to the top of the charts
To me you were just a beautiful spirit
And girl you rocked my heart
Away

I didn't know you were famous
Strumming to the top of the charts
To me you were just a beautiful spirit
And girl you rocked my heart
Away

◎

CALIFORNIA GIRL

We drive that cool coastal highway
Warm breeze, green palms
Another classic SoCal day
In the land of surf and songs

See the blue Pacific Ocean
Sparkling in the sun
We're on our way
Living the dream
Ans there's still so much to be done

Feel how life just opens
As we discover each others' worlds
Now everything is possible
And she's my California Girl
My California Girl

We've hiked the hidden canyons
Found the secrets at Crystal Cove
Explored the towns and mountains
And wondered at the stars above

Down the cliffs, along the coastline
We walk on the golden sand
I feel my heart healing
With the touch of her hand

Feel how life just opens
As we discover each others' worlds
Now everything is possible
And she's my California Girl
My California Girl

From Corona to Capistrano
Laguna out to the piers
She looks at me
With that smile and those eyes
Yeah, there's something special here

And in a moment of meditation
As i walk along the beach
I can feel the good vibrations
See all my dreams within reach

Feel how life just opens
As we discover each others' worlds
Now everything is possible
And she's my California Girl
My California Girl

Feel how life just opens
As we discover each others' worlds
Now everything is possible
And she's my California Girl
My California Girl

◎

HOLLYWOOD IS DEAD

Narration: *"...And in the news tonight, the death of movies. The apparent cause is suicide..."*

Turn it off
And step outside
A world awaits for you

All the distraction
They just want your reaction
All your money
And your soul, too

It's all illusion
They're creating a confusion
Got to get back
To what is true

Hollywood is Dead
Hollywood is Dead
Hollywood is Dead
Hollywood is Dead

Turn it off
The fake and make believe
Feel the real Life inside of you

They keep showing guns and violence
They'll sell sex, sex, sex
And crime
It's all about the bottom line

They'll fool your eyes
And trick your brain
And steal your money
And your life, two hours at a time

Hollywood is Dead
Hollywood is Dead
Hollywood is Dead
Hollywood is Dead

Give it up
The fascination with celebrities
Overpaid, acting like fools

Another sequel
Another 2 Star Bomb
All Publicity, so little Creativity
Trying to make you think it's cool

There's so much more
To the Universe
Than a mansion, car, and pool

Hollywood is Dead
Hollywood is Dead
Hollywood is Dead
Hollywood is Dead

Narration: "One must wonder..Is this the best our Civilization can offer?"

Hollywood is Dead
Hollywood is Dead
Hollywood is Dead
Hollywood is Dead

◎

NO ONE STILL KNOWS YOU

No one still knows you
Try to take that in
You came, a kid from outside Chicago
Years you've tried, everything you can

Yeah, you always were a Salesman
Promoting, selling mostly your self
And you might've met the Devil
Oh, but you would never tell

You always wanted to be "famous"
You've done everything you could
Steal a show or make a vid
Or click your latest post
And where's all that got you now?

No one still knows you
Try to take that in
You moved out to L.A. to make your big break
Now years, you've tried every trick you can

Today, your latest post is all about you
Careful, only what you want them to see
Remember, I was your good friend once, long ago
But saw the parts of you that you won't dare to see

Of course, you were never anyone
Anyone, except who you are
Yet you kept changing your name, chasing all those illusions
Long ago, you lost your own star
Your true star

But same as always, you keep trying
While you're lying to yourself
Still so desperate to be famous
Caught in a kind of hell

Years...
No one still knows you
Though there are friends gone, left behind
But that would take you being honest with yourself
Those are keys you'll never find

No one still knows you
No one still knows you
No one still knows you
No one still knows you

◎

TEMPORARY TRENDS

Temporary trends
T.V.
Empty images
Hourglass figures on the perfumed pages
Simply psychological stimuli
The power of suggestion
To enforce a lie

We've got too much distraction
On no big deal
And the Advertisements
That can make us feel
As if we'll never have enough
We know better
Time to call their bluff

Who do we admire?
I mean really admire
Let's set our sights a little higher
Above the dollars
And designer desires

We've got the hot shot actor hired to play a scene
And the make-up models in the magazines
Acting sexy
Acting tough
Don't be fooled
It's time to call their bluff

Temporary trends
T.V.
Empty images
Hourglass figures on the perfumed pages
Simply psychological stimuli
The power of suggestion
To enforce a lie

Who do we admire?
I mean really admire
Let's set our sights a little higher
Above the dollars
And designer desires

Who do we admire?
I mean really admire
Let's set our sights a little higher
Above the dollars
And designer desires

◎

BLUE JAY WAY

I have visions
Of a special place
With my girl
On Blue Jay Way

Feel the dreams
Golden memories
Make it real
Got to believe

Cruise along that coast
Down by the sea
Time to seize the day
All that can be

A better life
Touched with grace
With my girl
On Blue Jay Way

In a classic Porsche
We take a drive
Remember what it's like
To feel alive

Reach the dreams
And begin again
In the golden sunlight
Feel the wind

A better life
Touched with grace
With my girl
On Blue Jay Way

Feel the dreams
Golden memories
Make it real
Got to believe

Cruise along that coast
Down by the sea
Time to seize the day
All that can be

A better life
Touched with grace
With my girl
On Blue Jay Way

A better life
Touched with grace
With my girl
On Blue Jay Way

◎

AMBER EYES

She awakens in the morning
When the light is soft and golden
And the ocean is so still
It reflects the endless sky

Red sun on distant mesas
Breaks cool across the hills
Comes shining through her window
As she opens up
Her amber eyes

She arises with the turning
Of the Earth, in its glory
As she calls upon her ancestors
For wisdom and a guide

As she looks into the future
For she is the deepest spirit
Connected to all nature
And the tapestry of life

She is the cycle of the seasons
Of birth and death and rebirth
She is the wisdom of all women
She knows everything is One

She is a healer
She's a dancer
She is selfless in her giving
She feels the truth of loving
In her time beneath the sun

Now the sun is breaking golden
On the mountains in the morning
On the hills of manzanitas
With the scent of wild sage

As she walks down by the ocean
With the wisdom of the ages
Love is the key to living
And love is like the waves

So she awakens in the morning
When the light is soft and golden
And the ocean is so still
It reflects the endless sky

Red sun on distant mesas
Breaks cool across the hills
Comes shining through her window
As she opens up
Her amber eyes

◎

FALLINGSTAR

I could make the people laugh out loud
No one ever saw me cry
The whole world knows my name
Yet I could still feel so alone inside

Moments of brilliance
Up in the spotlight, stage and screens
All the talent I had I gave
But the pain that laughter hides, no one sees

Fallingstar
Fallingstar
Fallingstar

Fallingstar
Fallingstar
Fallingstar

Fallingstar
Fallingstar
Fallingstar

So high is the price for fame
It's more elusive to find love
All that attention doesn't save the soul
For the sorrow to rise above

After the lights burn bright and go down
And the laughter starts to fade
No one's there to hear the sound
Of the silence in the shade

Fallingstar
Fallingstar
Fallingstar

Fallingstar
Fallingstar
Fallingstar

Fallingstar
Fallingstar
Fallingstar

Oh, the fragile interplay
Between the comic and the tragic
Somewhere in the act, that dance
Sometimes there's the magic

Moments of brilliance
But it can be sad to be the clown
Shining like the brightest star
Yet feeling like the sun is going down

Fallingstar
Fallingstar
Fallingstar

Fallingstar
Fallingstar
Fallingstar

Fallingstar
Fallingstar
Fallingstar

Fallingstar
Fallingstar
Fallingstar

Fallingstar
Fallingstar
Fallingstar

Fallingstar
Fallingstar
Fallingstar

◎

HOLLYWOOD 2.0

Oh, they'll attract you
And distract you
And refract you
Until you lose your soul

All the screens and streaming
Steals your true dreaming
All they are is illusion
Nothing's what it seems

Hollywood is a business
All about the money, honey
They never cared
About you or I

You could turn it off
But you're addicted
That's how they trick you
Keep you hypnotized

They don't want you
To find out the truth, no
Behind their stories
It's all a lie

Oh, they'll attract you
And distract you
And refract you
Until you lose your soul

Another social media post
Taking your precious time
Led away from living and learning
Days clicked away

Until years are wasted
Watching day by day
You could've been doing so much more
With the gift of Life

You could turn it off
But you're addicted
That's how they trick you
Keep you hypnotized

You could be outdoors
Exploring the whole world
Real life is better
Than movies and CGI

◉

THEY LIE

They lie, they do
They lie
While they're smiling straight at you

With clever turns of phrases
They talk as if they know
Pretend to believe what they say
Make it sound true
It's all for show

See them on the screens
Speeches well prepared
Acting with their faces
To make you think they care

How they slyly pick the points
To weight their own cases
Bending the truth
To win their races

They lie, they do
They lie
While they're smiling straight at you

It's a media world now
Forget science and facts
Hollywood and politics are big business
Mostly done behind our backs

They advertise and raise millions
Funding their campaigns
Making out like bandits
And pointing to others for to blame

They come in every color
They don't all wear suits and ties
One thing they have in common
Hard to hear, but it's real

They lie, they do
They lie
While they're smiling straight at you

Some are inside corporations
And behind the party lines
Or protesting right or left
So short sighted they are blind

Careful if you question their views
They'll fight for the deals they've done
They say they don't hate, but they'll debate
Their lawyers are deadly as guns

You could count all their sins
But they won't go to hell
As long as you're swayed and watch the shows
Vote them into office
And buy what they sell

They lie, they do
They lie
While they're smiling straight at you

Their decisions have an impact
There's a cost to their way of being
Our children, generations, and Nature pays
Everything we're not seeing

Another forest gone
Another place to drill
Our oceans are now poisoned
As long as their pockets are getting filled

Keep the funding coming in
Any way they can
It's all a means to an end
Put our future at risk
Beat the competition
As long as their party wins

They lie, they do
They lie
While they're smiling straight at you

They lie, they do
They lie
While they're smiling straight at you

◎

DANCING WITH THE FANTASY

Dancing with the fantasy
Dancing with the dreams
Dancing with the spirits
Feel the flow of energy

Dancing with an open heart
Dancing with the rhythms
Push the bounds of reality
Seeking out new visions

Dancing true, with pure love
Dancing with cool motions
Reaching out to the earth and sky
And the waves out on the oceans

Dancing with the fantasy
Dancing with the fantasy
Dancing with the fantasy
Dancing with the fantasy

Dancing with the fantasy
Dancing with the dreams
Dancing with the spirits
Feel the flow of energy

Dancing with the fantasy
Dancing on the sliver screen
Dancing in the lights all night
Shaking up the scene

Dancing with emotions
Now's the time for healing
Dancing to your strong heart beat
Destiny revealing

Dancing with the fantasy
Dancing with the fantasy
Dancing with the fantasy
Dancing with the fantasy

◉

PACIFIC OCEAN BLUE

I want to walk down by the coastline
Pacific Ocean blue
Stand once more on that golden shore
Heart filled with dreams of you

I want to walk out on the sand
By the cliffs, down along the beach
Where you and I held hands
And felt all our dreams in reach

A precious time in our lives
When everything was new
But life it threw a change of plans
Now I'm alone in solitude

I want to walk down by the coastline
I want to feel the winds
Listen deep and try to find
A way to begin again

Like the California sunrise
Sky of golden hues
I want to walk down by the coastline
Pacific Ocean blue

I want to walk down by the coastline
Pacific Ocean blue
Watch the sun play on the waves
Like crystals shining true

I want to walk out on the sand
By the cliffs, down along the beach
Once again to find my way
And see new dreams to reach

This is the time in my life
To take all the love we knew
And not to break, but to fill my spirit
And continue to grow

I want to walk down by the coastline
I want to feel the winds
Listen deep and try to find
A way to begin again

Like the California sunrise
Sky of golden hues
I want to walk down by the coastline
Pacific Ocean blue

Like the California sunrise
Sky of golden hues
I want to walk down by the coastline
Pacific Ocean blue

◎

PACIFIC VIEW

See the sunrise
Watch the sands
Surf on the rocks
Awaken to the dreamland

Feel the Ocean waves
Endless blue
Reach far horizons
The day is new

Touch the piano keys
Strum the guitar
Find the rhythms beating
In your heart

Blue and golden
Feel your soul renewed
Gazing out to that
Pacific view

Mystic harmonies
As you play
The song of life
Time to seize the day

This is the place
To find your muse
Speaking in whispers
And nature's hues

Touch the piano keys
Strum the guitar
Find the rhythms beating
In your heart

Blue and golden
Feel your soul renewed
Gazing out to that
Pacific view

Step outside
Onto the balcony
Watch the sunset
And touch your dreams

See the starlight
Shimmering on the waves
Sparking like diamonds
Across the bay

Touch the piano keys
Strum the guitar
Find the rhythms beating
In your heart

Blue and golden
Feel your soul renewed
Gazing out to that
Pacific view

Blue and golden
Feel your soul renewed
Gazing out to that
Pacific view

◎

EXPERIENCE OF LIFE

This image exists
It is what it is
It's what it symbolizes
It's what you see

I take this idea
Then I take an action
Somehow, I create
What was not before

This
This experience of life
This
This experience of life
This
This experience of life
This
This experience of life

(Senses and perceptions
Lines of thought, raising questions
Leading us in new directions)

This image exists
It is not what it is not
What does it mean to you?
It is more than we know

There are changes
Patterns and interactions
It is not what it was
As you are not who you were

This
This experience of life
This
This experience of life
This
This experience of life
This
This experience of life

(Light, form, color
Red, Yellow, Blue
Illusions
Realities)

Is it what it is?
Or is it something else?
What are the relationships?
What do you see?

You are the audience
It is the object
You are now participant
What are your ideas?

This
This experience of life
This
This experience of life
This
This experience of life
This
This experience of life

◎

YOU ARE THE STAR

You are the star
You are, you are, you are
You are the star
You are, you are, you are

You've got to believe
You can reach and touch your dreams
You've got to believe
Everything is possible

It's never too late
To change the way you see
Find a new way
To profound discovery

You are the star
You are, you are, you are
You are the star
You are, you are, you are

No matter life's ups and downs
It's all a chance to grow
Keep your eyes and heart on your vision
Get on with the show

You are the star
You are, you are, you are
You are the star
You are, you are, you are

It's never too late
To change the way you see
Find a new way
To profound discovery

Every day
Is a step toward your dreams
Every day
Be the best that you can be

You are the star
You are, you are, you are
You are the star
You are, you are, you are

◎

SUCH A BEAUTIFUL THING

I was searching
I was so alone for so long
Now we are here
Together and with love so strong

We are born, we are here
For such a brief time
Living energy
Flowing in the dance of life

It's a beautiful thing
Walking side by side
Through this world with you

Such a beautiful thing
Walking side by side
Through this world with you

I was searching
Turned to look
But there was no one
'Til you appeared
And we came together
Circling with the moon and sun

Every day, we create
Our dreams
In the play of love and light
Ever since we met
It's like looking at the world
With new eyes

It's a beautiful thing
Walking side by side
Through this world with you

Such a beautiful thing
Walking side by side
Through this world with you

There will be a time
When we are gone
No longer here
As the dance of life
Carries on

But we were
And we are
Here, now, together
So it was
So it is
So we shall always be f
Forever

And so on and on and on
And on and on and on
And on and on and on
And on and on and on
And on and on and on
And on and on and on
And on and on and on
And on and on and on
And on and on and on and...

I was searching
I was so alone for so long
Now we are here
Together and with love so strong

So alive with the stars
In these precious years
Living energy
Moving with the Music of the Spheres

It's a beautiful thing
Walking side by side
Through this world with you

So beautiful, beautiful

Such a beautiful thing
Walking side by side
Through this world with you

So beautiful, beautiful

◉

5
REFLECTIONS OF THE CANYON

THE GETAWAY

Well I've burned some bridges
And I can't go back
Time to make a few changes
Find a new track
Now I'm rolling along
Still trying to find my way

Had some hard times
Lord, knows how I've tried
But all the work and distractions
Just fool the eye
Better watch my step
And all the tricks they play

Got to start where we are
Do what we can
To make it through
And plan the getaway

'Cause we can lose our spirits
In the search for gold
Can't you see them all
How they fit the mold?
All those illusions keep them hypnotized

Too long playing at the same old game
And there's danger when the days start to look the same
All the while
Real life is passing by

Got to start where we are
Do what we can
To make it through
And plan the getaway

But we can't just escape
Got to make it through
Another year
Stay strong, clear and true
All the wisdom shows
Real changes come from inside

Keep open to life
Every dawn to dusk
Keep on working hard
Do what we must
'Til we find the right space
And know when it's time

Got to start where we are
Do what we can
To make it through
And plan the getaway

Got to start where we are
Do what we can
To make it through
And plan the getaway

◎

ECHOES IN THE CANYON

Echoes in the canyon
Glimpses reach through time
Turn and look to nature
The river, cliffs, and sky

Sensing new vibrations
Standing outside, all alone
Feel reverberations
Off the water, sand, and stone

Whispers of the spirits
Transcending time and space
Rhythms of life's music
in this sacred place

Now, see the signs and circles
Beneath the stars at night
Bringing dreams and visions
Into dawn's sun-golden light

Echoes in the canyon
Speaking to you now
As you touch this life around you
You must decide the way you'll go

For there are witches
Who will steer you
Left or wrong or right
Others close will try to keep you
From your course and shining bright

Yet the path is there before you
That only you can see
Your dream and true heart guiding
As you choose who you must be

So from this moment forward
You must overcome old fears
Live the songs that are inside you
For all the world to hear

And so, joining with great others
All the stars who came before
The timeless music flowing
Now, sing the beauty that is yours

How the world it keeps on changing
All the billions in their homes
The music is for healing
Let's them know they're not alone

Echoes in the canyon
River, trees, and skies above
As Nature gives her secrets
Find the key to all is love

Echoes in the canyon
River, trees, and skies above
As Nature gives her secret
Find the key to all...
Is Love

◎

SOUTHERN WIND

And she runs
And she tries
And she makes it
Through the nights

To face the days' realities
All the pressures
She don't need

She's got to make the change
Make it someday
Just enough money
To get away

Yes, she knows it is time
To begin again
Go where the sun shines
On the Southern wind

She's got to make the change
Make it someday
Just enough money
To get away

Sometimes her dreams
Seem so far
Other times they're so close
She could touch the stars

She hears them calling
Sweet island sounds
Just a little while now
She'll be sailing down

Yes, she knows it is time
To begin again
Go where the sun shines
On the Southern wind

Yes, she knows it is time
To begin again
Go where the sun shines
On the Southern wind

◎

SET YOU FREE

Come on now
Gather 'round
Can you feel the energy?

Raise the torch up high
To the sky
Shine the light
Lady Liberty

Come on now
Let it set you free
Come on now
Let it set you free
Come on now
Let it set you free

Face the anger
With something stronger
Walk along
In the way of peace

Come on now
Let it set you free
Come on now
Let it set you free
Come on now
Let it set you free

Across all boundaries
To the highest mountains
Light a candle
To their memories

Come on now
Let it set you free
Come on now
Let it set you free
Come on now
Let it set you free

Come on now
Let it set you free
Come on now
Let it set you free
Come on now
Let it set you free

Come on now
Let it set you
Free
Free
Free

◎

SONGBIRD

There's a songbird who sang in Coconut Grove
She's a gypsy dancer with the words of a poet
She and her guitar
Can reach the soul

Down from Canada
She's a lady of the canyon
With a song for the roses
An artist's hands
Sketching in her lines
Of love, light and shadows

Hear the songbird singing
Singing in the sunrise
Songbird singing
Singing in the golden light

Hear the songbird singing
Singing in the evening
Songbird singing
Singing her songs so bright

Painting colors in sound
On a river so blue
That California sun can pull through
A strong woman of heart and mind
With her love of life so true

She's a sweet songbird with golden hair
Only know her through her music
As it fills the air
Floating like a breeze
With a voice so fair

Hear the songbird singing

Singing in the sunrise
Songbird singing
Singing in the golden light

Hear the songbird singing
Singing in the evening
Songbird singing
Singing her songs so bright

Hear the songbird singing
Singing in the sunrise
Songbird singing
Singing in the golden light

Hear the songbird singing
Singing in the evening
Songbird singing
Singing her songs so bright

◉

YOUNG HEART SEARCHING

Everybody know this is somewhere
But is it where you were meant to be?
You've had a good harvest for a year or two
But how quickly time fades away

Until you find yourself on a long, lost shore
Standing at the edge, on the beach
Whatever happened to all the dreams?
Always so near, yet just out of reach

So you keep on struggling through
The day to day fight
Hoping it will happen soon
Praying that tonight's the night

Only to be blinded
From the far side of the sun
So you keep going strong
Long may you run

Young heart searching
Through the haze
Young heart searching
To find the way

Young heart searching
Through the haze
Young heart searching
To find the way

Across America, around the world
Trough the bars and the stars
Comes a time to face the music
See who we truly are

Dreams never sleep
They keep flying
Like hawks and the doves
Repeating patterns of wars and peace
Like the emotions of love

And you respond and transition
While 'round the world, everybody's Rockin'
Yet they've forgotten the old ways
Hoping to land safe on the water

To rediscover life
All that is true
The gift of life is just like music
And every note is for you

Young heart searching
Through the haze
Young heart searching
To find the way

Young heart searching
Through the haze
Young heart searching
To find the way

And there is a song of Freedom
In all it's rigged glory
Beneath a harvest moon
With a song of the Angels

Amidst broken arrows and mirrors
Flashes of silver and gold
Signs of passion, being out in nature
Green forests, on the winds tales are told

We're still living with wars
All the dreams killed with chrome
Ears filled with noise
Writing lost letters home

Wishing for a better story
After High-Tech Chemical Years
Always, constant searching
For a Peace Trail

Feeling like a Visitor
Traveling all that is here
Reaching to the peaks of Colorado
Where the whispers are clear

◎

CARAVAN

The caravan is coming
How they follow, one by one
Hear the sound of the drumming
Led to the land of the setting sun

Covert maneuvers in the desert
Mining diamonds from the sand
A satellite spies below the surface
Where long ago the rivers ran

Shake, shake from the mountains
Clouds roll across the sky
Fire dance in the fountain
Gone, in the blink of an eye

Drill for black gold in the tundra
Trade to fuel economies
Somewhere, deep in a jungle
There is life we'll never see

Piano play staccato
To lamenting violins
All these voices tomorrow
Sing on a silent wind

Shake, shake from the mountains
Clouds roll across the sky
Fire dance in the fountain
Gone, in the blink of an eye

Shake, shake from the mountains
Clouds roll across the sky
Fire dance in the fountain
Gone, in the blink of an eye

◎

VOICE OF A GREAT SPIRIT

I was all alone
Driving through the night
No one at my side
Yet I could feel you there

I was all alone
Traveling down that road
To somewhere I must go
I could feel you there

And I can hear you now
As I'm strumming my guitar
Singing to the stars
I can hear you now

The voice of a great spirit
I'm on a path all my own
Against the odds, and to myself staying true
The voice of a great spirit
Bringing wisdom all around
May there always shine stars and the sun ahead of you

And I can see you now
Traveling down that road
Somewhere fine to go
I can see you now

I can see you now
And I just have to smile
Because I know you're out there somewhere
Running free

Can you hear me now?
Remember every song
We sang together all along
In harmony

The voice of a great spirit
On a path all our own
Against the odds, and to ourselves staying true
The voice of a great spirit
Bringing wisdom all around
May there always shine stars and the sun ahead of you

Oh, I can feel it now
Glimpses beyond sound
In the colors and the light
Feel the energy

I can see it now
Across the mountains and the sky
Opening up my eyes
To the great mystery

The voice of a great spirit
On a path all our own
Against the odds, and to ourselves staying true
The voice of a great spirit
Bringing wisdom all around
May there always shine stars and the sun ahead of you

The voice of a great spirit
On a path all our own
Against the odds, and to ourselves staying true
The voice of a great spirit
Bringing wisdom all around
May there always shine stars and the sun ahead of you

◎

IF I KNEW NOW WHAT I KNEW THEN

In the evenings that I came to you
I was astray out in the rain, running for cover
You took me in your arms without my saying a thing
And we fell into dreams, beside each other
Embracing the pains from a world outside
And replacing them with the light in one another
We came so close
And touched as lovers

If I'd only known you wanted more than friendship
Because today it is clear you tried to tell me, somehow
Now I've been told not to dwell on what could have been
But, oh, if I knew then what I know now

In the evenings that you came to me
You were astray out in the cold and running for cover
I held you in my arms. We didn't say a thing
And we fell into dreams, beside each other
Embracing the pains from a world outside
And replacing them with the light in one another
We came so close
And touched as lovers

If together we'd held on another instant
The distance would have ceased to be forever
We never should have hid behind our shyness
For what lay just beyond could only have led to paradise
One step too far, to take at the time

Since you've gone, I've come to miss your gentleness
And I've been told not to dwell on what could have been
The way I see it, we both gained a friend
But, oh, if I knew now what I knew then

If I knew now, what I knew then

◎

REDISCOVERY

I've been too long in this city
Working for the money
Yet, somehow always feeling
This is not where I was born to be

Let us go exploring
In the country or by the sea
Find another, better way
Out of a dream or a memory

Let us set out early
Walk the forest, by the steams
Hear the land and waters calling
And remember how to live

Let us feel our footsteps
Soft upon the earth
Hiking that old, winding trail
A path back to our hearts

Let us go exploring
In the country or by the sea
Find another, better way
Rediscovery

Let us go exploring
In the country or by the sea
Find another, better way
Rediscovery

I've been too long in this city
Working for the money
Yet somehow always feeling
This is not where I was born to be

Let us go out driving
Down by the crystal coast
See the blue waters shining
The waves crashing on the rocks

Let us set out early
Walk along the sand
Feel the love between us
Here, come and take my hand

Let us look to the horizon
To the edge of infinity
Share this time together
As we create our destiny

Let us go exploring
In the country or by the sea
Find another, better way
Rediscovery

Let us go exploring
In the country or by the sea
Find another, better way
Rediscovery

◎

UNIVERSAL MAN

I'm a universal man
Some of you won't understand
I listen to the spirit guides
Connecting with the Earth and Sky

Up to watch the golden sunrise
Opening my heart and mind
Feeling waves of energy
Reaching to infinity

Go hiking through the forest green
Remembering what it is to be One
With the mountains, waters, and trees
Recalling how to be free

I'm a universal man
We walk together, hand in hand
She and I go along the beach
Feeling the love within our reach

And from the edge of the sands
I set out from the lands
Sailing the Oceans and Seas
Sailing the stars and galaxies

Into the great mysteries
Seeing all that is and can be
Traveling through Space and Time
Feel Life dancing in the light

I'm a universal man
Some of you won't understand
I listen to the spirit guides
Connecting with the Earth and Sky

I'm a universal man
I see Nature's caravan
I feel the rhythms and the breath
Of planet Earth, may she be blessed

I'm a universal man
We walk together, hand in hand
I see the signals and the signs
We walk in touch with the divine

We go in peace and travel light
All the Universe is right
Here
Now

◎

BE READY FOR PEACE

Keep your head down
There's still fighting at the border
Hear the crack of gunfire around the corner
Who knows where the next bomb will explode?

And there's a flash of fire in the night
Years, and there's no end in sight
Just fears, and souls filled with anger
Aimed straight at taking lives of strangers

Beliefs and faith and holy signs
Your beliefs can make you blind

Oh, to hope when all hope is gone
Turn our eyes toward the sun

Be ready for Peace
When it comes
Be ready for Peace
When it comes

Feel the blast as the windows all are shattered
To the winds, thousands of lives are scattered
You better run, if you want to stay alive

Bullets fly an inch past your ear
A woman's cry, and children's tears
Step back and see the world we've made
More than earth can sustain

The rivers poison, the forests gone
And the Wars are raging on

Yet I see a day when will it come
When men at last lay down their guns

Be ready for Peace
When it comes
Be ready for Peace
When it comes

Be ready for Peace
When it comes
Be ready for Peace
When it comes

Be ready for Peace
When it comes
Be ready for Peace
When it comes

◎

SPIRIT WARRIOR

This is the end
This is the beginning
A time to trust
A heart that is willing

This is the edge
Between the past and the future
All that came before
On a Quest that is new

This is the place
Both empty and full
Standing at the portal
Looking into the void

I've come this far
To seek and to find
Aa a Spirit Warrior
Touching the Divine

Aa a Spirit Warrior
Touching the Divine

This is a death
Letting go of the old
This is the change
That's needed to grow

This is the step
Out into the Unknown
Reaching Dreams and Visions
Of infinite potential

There's no turning back
From the pain, I've cried my tears
I must challenge and face
My deepest fears

I've come this far
To seek and to find
As a Spirit Warrior
Touching the Divine

As a Spirit Warrior
Touching the Divine

This is the courage
I must try, though might fall
To take actions and to fail
Get up, and keep going on

Rising out of all ashes
Like the great phoenix
Spread my wings in the sunlight
And gathering strength

This is the Life
The life I must lead
To keep going forwards
To realize my dreams

I've come this far
To seek and to find
As a Spirit Warrior
Touching the Divine

As a Spirit Warrior
Touching the Divine

This is the end
This is the beginning
A time to trust
A heart that is willing

This is the Life
The life I must lead
To keep going forwards
To realize my dreams

This is the Life
The life I must lead
To break free
And go beyond
To my true destiny

I've come this far
To seek and to find
As a Spirit Warrior
Touching the Divine

As a Spirit Warrior
Touching the Divine

◎

Craig Enger was born in Maryland, educated at Syracuse and Johns Hopkins University, and is a an IT business consultant, investor, writer, artist, and musician. He is a songwriter and producer of several albums including COASTLINE, WISH, SAILING, RUSTIC SERENITY, and more. He is author of the fiction thrillers TEN DARK TALES and THE PLEASURE DOME, the poetry books DREAM VISIONS, SONGS of HEART & SPIRIT, SONGS of ART & COURAGE, and co-author of the inspiring nonfiction book AMERICA SPEAKS. Between projects he pursues \numerous interests and world travels.